My Body as a Place of Peace

a sensory and reflective journal

Created by R.S. Britton

with love for those learning to
feel at home in their own body

My Body as a Place of Peace

By R.S. Britton

Copyright © 2025 R.S. Britton
ISBN: 978-1-300-14127-3

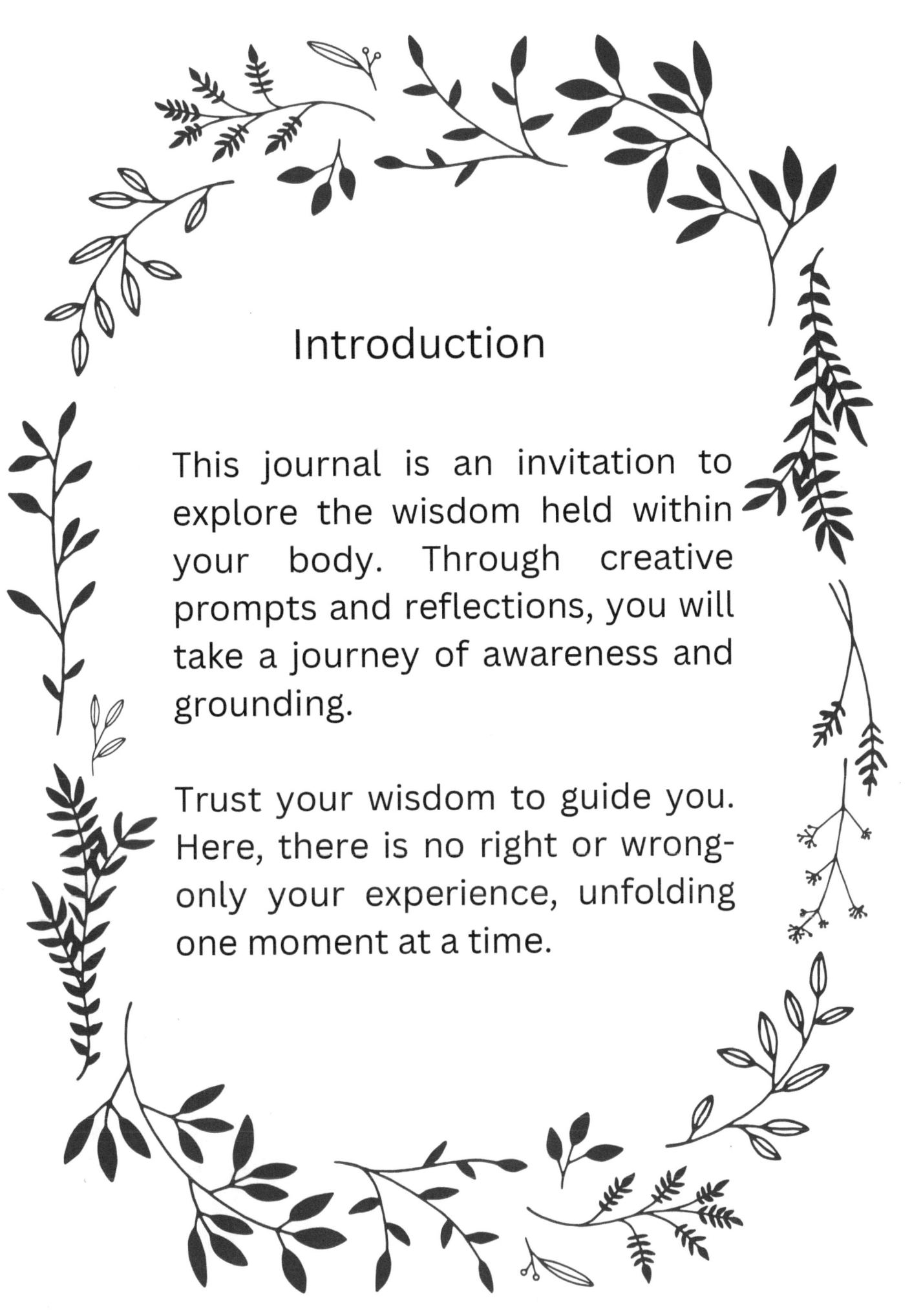

Introduction

This journal is an invitation to explore the wisdom held within your body. Through creative prompts and reflections, you will take a journey of awareness and grounding.

Trust your wisdom to guide you. Here, there is no right or wrong—only your experience, unfolding one moment at a time.

These are my eyes

My eyes know how to widen, soften, and rest.

They've seen beauty, pain, and everything in between.

My eyes show where my attention lingers, and they can choose which direction to look.

What do my eyes find beautiful?

Draw your eyes and something they see.

This is my energy

My energy knows how to rise, fade, and return.

Some days it sparks. Some days it fades.
My energy flows like sunlight through trees –
sometimes bright, sometimes hidden.
It isn't always loud or fast,
but it is always mine.

What is the shape of my energy today?

Draw your energy as a color, motion or flame.

This is my back

My back knows how to carry, support, and release.

It carries what I do not see.
It holds tension I forget to name.
My back has held me upright through long days
and curled in quiet when I needed rest.
It remembers every weight I've tried to ignore.

What does my back need to let go of?

Draw your back or something it's carrying.

This is my code

My code knows how to rewrite itself when I grow.

Some of it was written by others.
Some by time.
Some, I now right myself.

What beliefs, patterns, or truths have you outgrown- and what new ones are you choosing?

Draw your code as symbols, lines, or shapes.

This is my breath

My breath knows how to soften, steady, and stay.

It comes and goes without asking.
A quiet rhythm beneath everything I do.
My breath knows how to soften pain,
how to carry me through stillness or fear.
It is the part of me that always stays.

What does my breath feel like right now?

Draw your breath as a wave or a cloud.

I am...

This is me.

Draw yourself lovingly.

This is my balance

My balance knows how to pause, hold, and play.

I have not always understood it. At times I've been without it, it felt as though balance might never return. But it has, as balance does. Slowly. Subtly.

How does my balance show up for me?

Draw how you see your balance.

These are my ears

My ears know how to listen, notice, and hold stillness.

They listen even when I don't mean to.
To laughter down the hall.
To wind through the trees.
To silence that speaks louder than sound.
My ears open me to the world – and to myself.

What do my ears hear when the world is quiet?

Draw your ears and the sounds they hold.

This is my anchor

This steadies me when the wind rises.
It may be quiet. Small.
But it keeps me from drifting too far.

Draw what keeps you safe, grounded, or held.

This is what my body is trying to tell me right now

It speaks in tension, in restlessness, in stillness. In the ache, the breath, the deep exhale. My tiredness is not laziness, my tension is not failure. I speak in warmth, in aches, in stillness.

Are you listening?

Draw how your body feels, not looks.

This is my belly

My belly knows how to fill, soften, and nourish.

It is not loved enough but my belly is where I feel, where hunger, instinct, and emotion all live together.
It takes in what I need, and lets the rest go.
My belly does not have to be the same to always be loved.

How can I be kinder to my belly?

Draw your belly and what it holds.

These are my legs

My legs know how to stand, move, and carry me forward.

They've carried me farther than I remember.
Up hills. Through pain. Into joy.
My legs have felt strong, and they've felt tired,
but they have always moved me forward.
They are part of my strength.

Where have my legs taken me that I'm grateful for?

Draw your legs or a journey they helped you make.

This is my movement

My movement knows how to shift, stretch, and return.

It doesn't have to be big to be real.
My movement lives in stretches, shifts, and small dances.
It's how I reach, how I return.
Even in stillness, I move toward myself.

How does my body ask to move today?

Draw your movement - as lines, shapes or a path.

These are my hands

They've held so many things.
Warm mugs, sleepy heads, long letters.
Your hands remember more than you
think. They shape, soothe, protect, and
reach.

What have your hands carried that
shaped who you are?

Draw your hands and what they hold.

This is my soul

My soul knows how to listen beneath the noise.

The part of me untouched by time.
Older than fear. Deeper than memory.
It speaks in feelings I don't have words for.

When have you felt most like your full self?

Draw your soul in motion.

This is my heart

My heart knows how to ache, open, and hold joy.

It beats for me, even when I'm not listening.
It holds joy, ache, hope, and memory- all layered
together like a secret song.
My heart has broken and healed in ways no one
else can see.

What is my heart carrying right now?

Draw your heart, or the feelings it holds.

I am...

Not a single thing, but many.
Not a final answer, but a living question.

What "are you" right now?

Draw yourself as you are.

This is my voice

My voice knows how to rise, retreat, and return.

It has spoken when I was brave.
It has gone quiet when I was afraid.
My voice holds truths I haven't yet learned how
to say.
Still, it rises - gentle or strong -
trying to find its way back to me.

What has my voice been waiting to speak?

Draw your voice as a shape or a sound

This is my light

My light knows how to glow in silence - not for show, but because it must.

It's what I carry through the dark.
Sometimes a lantern. Sometimes just a spark.
But it's always mine - and always enough.

When have you shined, even when the world was dim?

Draw your light as a glow, a sun, or a moon.

These are my values

My values know how to walk away when something costs too much of me.

My memories know how to echo, teach, and shift.
They hold me steady when everything else shifts.
Not rules - but roots.
They whisper, "This is who you are, even when no one else is watching."

What do you stand for, even in silence?

Draw your values as stones, symbols or seeds.

This is a map of me

Trace the places where you feel steady. The ones that still ache. The places you hide, and the ones you've learned to love.

Draw your inner landscape. Label what matters.

This is my spark

That sudden flicker.
That yes inside the chest.
It's small but electric, and it knows how to begin
again.

Draw what your spark looks like.

These are my memories

My memories know how to echo, teach, and shift.

They do not always arrive the same way.
Some are loud. Some are gentle.
My memories have shaped how I move, what I fear, and who I love.
And still, I am not only what I remember.

Which memories feel close today?

Draw a memory - or what it gave you.

This is my sleep

My sleep knows how to gather, restore, and protect.

It doesn't always come easy.
But when it does, it gathers me in quiet arms.
My sleep is where I soften, where I release the day. It is a kind of return –
to stillness, to safety, to self.

What helps my body feel ready to rest?

Draw your sleep as a blanket, dream or a space.

I am...

What are you today?
Satisfied? Loved? Happy?

Draw yourself today.

These are my feet

My feet know how to ground, balance, and stay.

They've carried me across quiet mornings and hurried afternoons. They've danced in soft grass and curled beneath warm blankets. Even when tired, even when sore- they've never stopped moving forward.

Where have my feet taken me?

Draw your feet and the places they remember.

This is my skin

My skin knows how to feel, remember, and protect.

It holds me together. It feels the sun, the wind, the brush of kindness.
My skin remembers every touch- the ones that comforted and the ones that hurt.
It is my first boundary, and my first connection.

What has my skin been asked to hold?

Draw your skin as a texture, memory or boundary.

This is my shadow

My shadow knows how to follow, reflect, and stay.

It follows me, even when I turn away.
My shadow holds what I hide - the fears, the anger, the ache.
But it is part of me.
And when I face it gently, it softens.

What part of me is asking to be seen?

Draw your shadow or something you've hidden.

This is my passion

It burns in me. Not politely. Not quietly.

It's the thing I'd chase through fire to feel alive.
It doesn't wait for permission.
It growls, it pulses, it dares.
When it speaks, it becomes a force.
When I ignore it, it finds its way out.

What would you fight for, even if no one believed in it but you?

Draw the shape of your passion.

This is my personality

My personality knows how to color outside the lines, and mean it.

It's not a mask- it's a constellation.
Flashes of laughter, quiet obsessions, contradictions I've made peace with.
This is how I move through the world.

What makes you YOU, even in a crowded room?

Draw your personality as a shape, color, or collage.

These are my scars

My scars know how to heal, remember, and continue.

They do not ask to be seen.
They are stories my body remembers - of pain,
of healing, of survival.
Some are quiet. Some still ache.
But every scar says: I made it through.

What have my scars taught me?

Draw your scars or the strength that followed.

This is my silence

Not empty- but full of breath, pause, and space
to return to myself.
In the quiet, I remember who I am.
It is my shelter, my soft boundary, my breath
between thoughts.

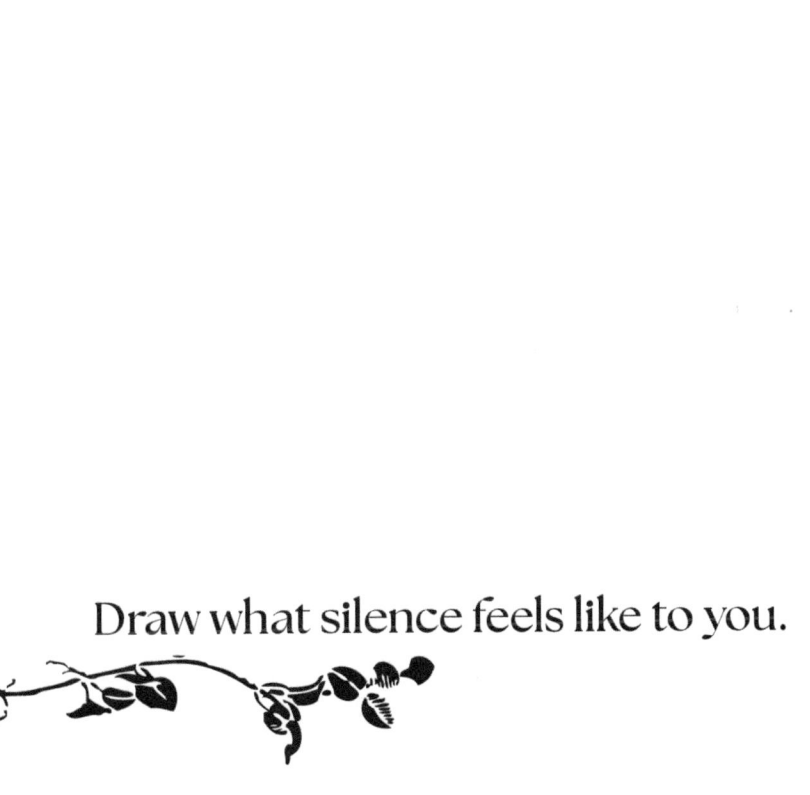

Draw what silence feels like to you.

This is my stillness

My stillness knows how to hold, soften, and calm.

It sits beneath the chatter, the restlessness, the noise. My stillness is where I pause, where I regather what's scattered. It is where I take a breath and remember -

What helps my body find stillness?

Draw your stillness as a space, a shape, or feeling.

This is me today

Not yesterday's version. Not tomorrow's hope. Just the me that showed up right now- tired, fierce, soft, uncertain. Here.

Draw the version of you that arrived today.

This is my peace

Peace isn't the absence of noise.
It is not a place I go. It is something I let in.
It lives between heartbeats, in the space after a
deep exhale.
It settles in like a soft rain after the storm.

My peace might be fragile – but it is real.

Draw what peace looks like to you.

This is where I am

I do not need to be finished to be whole.
I do not need to be healed to be at peace.
I am exactly where I am meant to be - for now.

What did I learn about my body in these pages?

You do not have to become anything else.
You are already becoming.

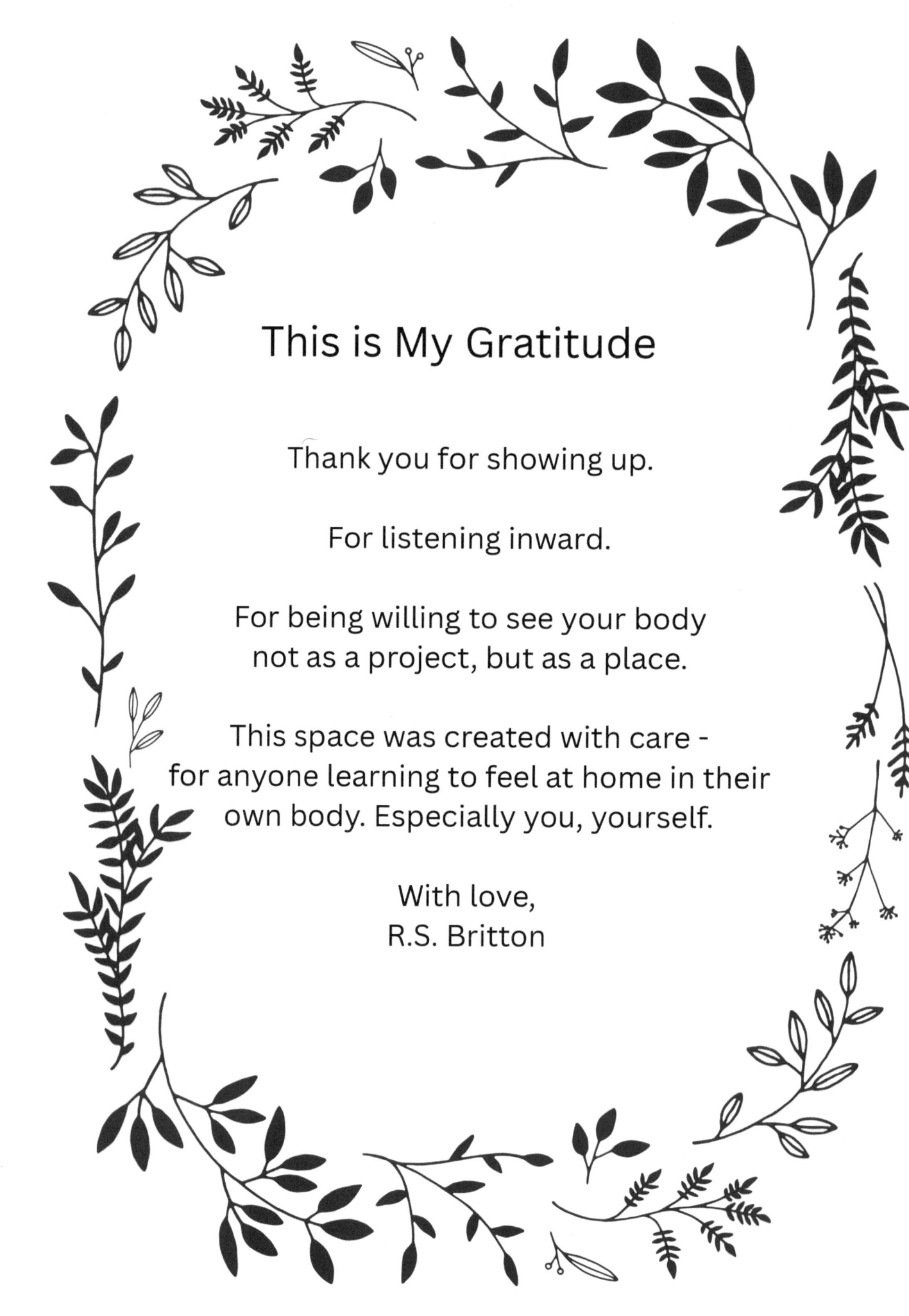

This is My Gratitude

Thank you for showing up.

For listening inward.

For being willing to see your body
not as a project, but as a place.

This space was created with care -
for anyone learning to feel at home in their
own body. Especially you, yourself.

With love,
R.S. Britton